STUDY GUIDE

UNLEASHED

HOW TO TURN YOUR MESSAGE INTO IMPACT

Cover design by: Joe DeLeon
Cover photo by: Xenia Design

ISBN: 978-1-954089-04-4   1 2 3 4 5 6 7 8 9 10

Printed in the United States of America

STUDY GUIDE

UNLEASHED

HOW TO TURN YOUR MESSAGE INTO IMPACT

MARTIJN VAN TILBORGH

INSPIRE

CONTENTS

INTRODUCTION

Reflect and Discuss

Martijn writes, "One thing I've discovered in my life is that the abundance of God is a lot bigger than we think."

Respond

Have you embraced this statement on an intellectual level? Explain your answer.

_____

_____

_____

_____

_____

Do you truly believe this statement? Why or why not?

_____

_____

_____

_____

_____

Does your current reality match what you believe?

_____

_____

_____

_____

_____

Reflect and Discuss

Martijn writes, "Your mind has the power to make you believe that your current state of life is acceptable, even though you know better."

Why do you think people often settle for second best?

_____

_____

_____

_____

_____

_____

Do you currently find yourself settling in any areas of your life? What are they?

_____

_____

_____

_____

_____

_____

_____

Do you think it's more painful to pretend that we're living in all the abundance that God has for us, or to face the truth that we're not? Explain your answer.

_____

_____

_____

_____

_____

_____

What's one thing you hope to learn, or put into action, by the end of this study?

_____

_____

_____

_____

_____

_____

THIS STUFF IS REAL

Martijn reflects on how he transitioned from being thousands of dollars in debt to a place where God allowed him to prosper in his business. He examines the principles and actions that helped make the difference.

Read Chapter 1 in *Unleashed*

Respond

Have you ever experienced a season in your life similar to the one Martijn went through? What challenges did you face?

_____

_____

_____

_____

_____

_____

_____

How did this situation leave you feeling?

_____

_____

_____

_____

_____

_____

_____

Respond

Beyond the car, what does this testimony reveal about God's heart toward His children?

_____

_____

_____

_____

_____

_____

How does this knowledge affect the way you approach your problems, opportunities, and dreams?

_____

_____

_____

_____

_____

_____

Have you ever seen God do more than you've asked or imagined? How so?

_____

_____

_____

_____

_____

_____

Why do you think God delights in doing more than we ask or imagine?

_____

_____

_____

_____

_____

_____

IT'S ALL ABOUT STEWARDSHIP

*It is possible to live a life you love—
and make money while you're at it!
It all centers around how well you're
stewarding what God has given you.*

Read Chapter 2 in *Unleashed*

Respond

Whom do you know that stewards their resources (time, money, relationships, etc.) well? How have you seen abundance in this person's life as a result?

_____

_____

_____

_____

Deep down, do you believe you can live a life that you love—a life of significance and value—while still making money? Why or why not?

_____

_____

_____

_____

What key lessons do you take away from the Parable of the Talents?

_____

_____

_____

_____

Respond

Do you currently feel you are working within the "grace of your talent"? Explain your answer.

_____

_____

_____

_____

_____

_____

_____

We have to know our gifts before we can steward them well. Make a list of the talents and skills that God has given you.

_____

_____

_____

_____

_____

_____

_____

How might each of these gifts be utilized by God to provide for your financial situation? Be creative—list whatever possibilities come to mind.

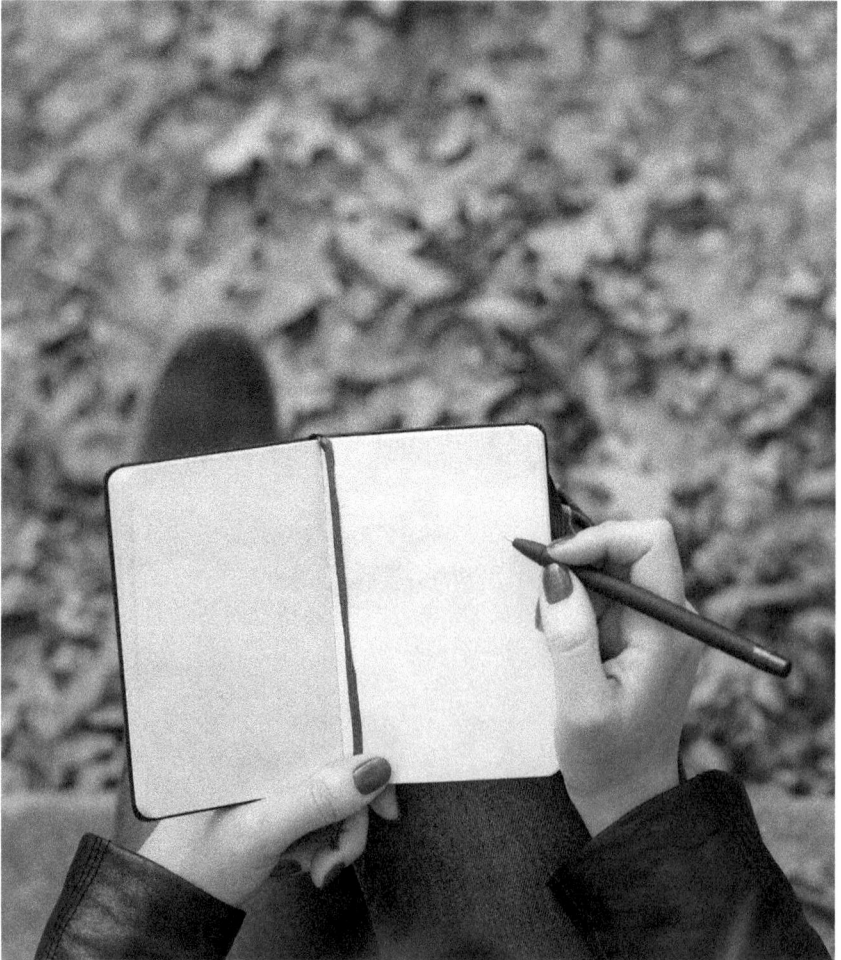

_____

_____

_____

_____

_____

_____

_____

_____

Reflect and Discuss

"Much of what we see God do throughout the Bible is content marketing. He is the world's best content marketer."

Respond

God brings His message to His market, all while engaging His audience. Think about a few stories from the Bible that demonstrate this content marketing. Which stories can you think of, and how do they show this at work?

_____

_____

_____

_____

_____

_____

What cost, or opposition, was involved in sharing the gospel—both for God and for those He called to help spread the message?

_____

_____

_____

_____

_____

_____

What does this tell you about the process of bringing your message to market?

_____

_____

_____

_____

_____

_____

Write a short prayer surrendering your talents to God. Commit to follow Him, and ask Him to prepare your heart for what He has next for you.

_____

_____

_____

_____

_____

_____

THE GREATEST INVENTION OF ALL TIME

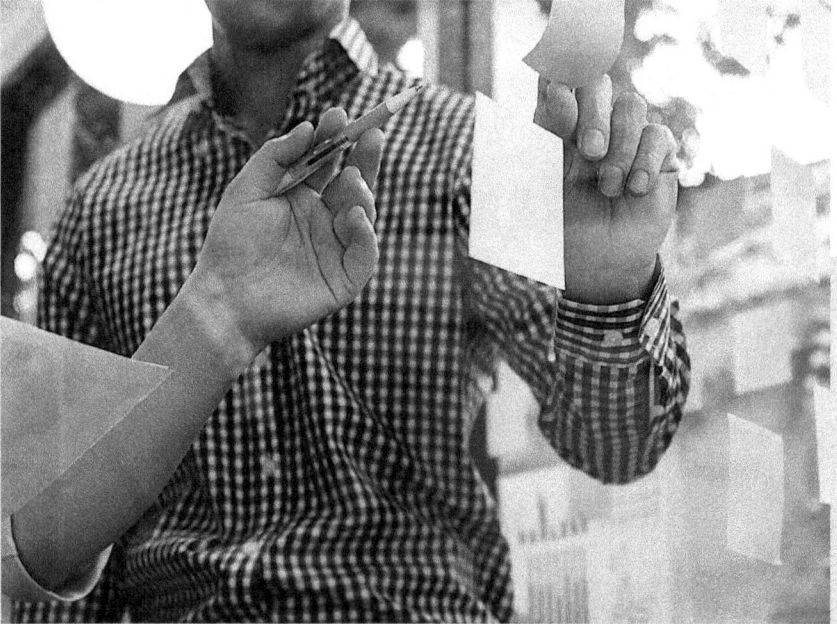

Cowboys rode for hours to catch their prey before barbed wire was invented. After that, they could rest easier, step outside, and select their dinner. We can apply the same strategic principle to our endeavors.

Read Chapter 3 in *Unleashed*

Respond

What do you think is the greatest invention of all time? Why?

_____

_____

_____

_____

In your own words, explain how "raising your own cattle" can help you maximize your potential.

_____

_____

_____

_____

What efforts are you currently making that could be minimized, or eliminated altogether, if you were to begin producing right where you are?

_____

_____

_____

_____

chapter 4

THE BEST WAY TO FISH

*It's possible to create an environment
so magnetic that your "fish"
will jump into your boat.*

Read Chapter 4 in *Unleashed*

Respond

What's your initial reaction to watching the fishing video?

_____

_____

_____

_____

What role do you think the ecosystem, the environment, played in the catch these men brought home?

_____

_____

_____

_____

How did they still need to prepare for the moment when the fish jumped into their boat?

_____

_____

_____

_____

_____

Respond

What's your initial reaction to watching the webinar video?

_____

_____

_____

_____

_____

_____

Martijn's team also had to prepare in order to create this moment. What preparation do you think went into this?

_____

_____

_____

_____

_____

_____

_____

What preparation might you still need to put into the process, even with an ecosystem ripe for making sales and marketing your message?

_____

_____

_____

_____

_____

_____

Do you have any final thoughts on this chapter and the principle we've just explored?

_____

_____

_____

_____

_____

_____

THE LAST THING YOU NEED IS A WEBSITE!

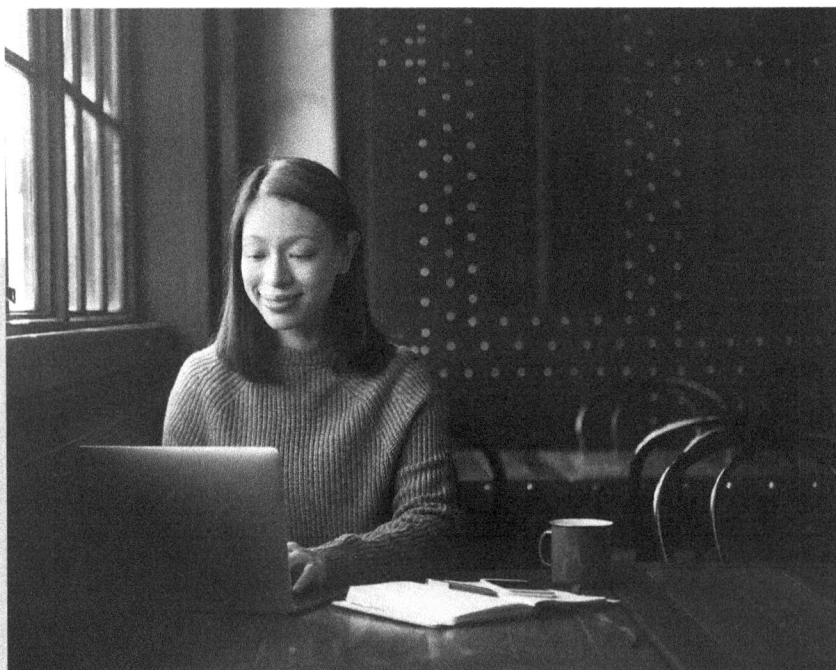

While websites are useful for some things, they should be the beginning of an ongoing relationship between you and your customers.

Read Chapter 5 in *Unleashed*

Reflect and Discuss

The prophet asked her a simple question: "Tell me, what do you have in your house?"

Respond

Why do you think Elijah asked the widow this question?

_____

_____

_____

_____

What resources do you currently have at your disposal that you may be overlooking?

_____

_____

_____

_____

What could you do with those resources to maximize your potential and profits?

_____

_____

_____

_____

_____

How does this limit the impact that websites offer you and your business?

_____

_____

_____

_____

_____

_____

Does this change your perspective of websites and other similar marketing tools? Why or why not?

_____

_____

_____

_____

_____

_____

This isn't to say websites are useless. What value could there still be in a website that is able to hold and retain a viewer's attention past the five-second mark?

_____

_____

_____

_____

_____

_____

_____

Respond

The first question people ask is, "Where am I?" How can you answer this question effectively on your webpage or website?

_____

_____

_____

_____

_____

_____

The second question people ask is, "What can I do here?" What options can you provide them within the first five seconds of their visit?

_____

_____

_____

_____

_____

_____

What steps do you most want your online visitors to take when they come to your website?

_____

_____

_____

_____

_____

_____

The third question people ask is, "Why should I do this with you?" What credibility do you have to offer them, and how can you show it quickly and effectively?

_____

_____

_____

_____

_____

_____

Respond

Why do you think trust is integral to the buying-and-selling process?

_____

_____

_____

_____

_____

_____

Recall a time when you made an online purchase. What did you need to know, feel, or understand before pulling out your credit or debit card?

_____

_____

_____

_____

_____

_____

Are you currently able to further the conversation with your customers on your own terms? Explain your answer.

_____

_____

_____

_____

_____

_____

_____

Respond

How have you seen this played out with your own customer base? How have you needed to develop those you sell to before they're ready?

_____

_____

_____

_____

_____

_____

The stepping stones of your sales cycle will slowly develop your leads into the perfect customers you want. What stepping stones are currently at play in your organization?

_____

_____

_____

_____

_____

_____

_____

What stepping stones would you like to implement, or enhance, in your sales cycle? Remember, these can be in-person, over-the-phone, or online steps.

_____

_____

_____

_____

_____

_____

_____

chapter 6

LIFE CYCLE MARKETING

Marketing is supposed to render a profit. If you have to ask yourself how much marketing you can afford, you're doing something wrong.

Read Chapter 6 in *Unleashed*

Reflect and Discuss

"The problem is that traditional advertising and marketing don't work. They're inefficient, expensive, and typically, not sustainable long-term."

Respond

Are you currently making a profit from your marketing endeavors?

_____

_____

_____

_____

How have you seen traditional advertising be counterintuitive?

_____

_____

_____

_____

Do you resonate with the frustration that many marketers feel at the high percentage of leads lost? Explain your answer.

_____

_____

_____

_____

Respond

Why do you think our focus is more centered on making customers
and not on retaining them?

_____

_____

_____

_____

_____

_____

_____

Do you currently have customer-retention strategies in place?

_____

_____

_____

_____

_____

_____

"Life Cycle Marketing interacts with your leads and clients in context of where they are on their journey of becoming your perfect customers."

Respond

For each of the seven phases of the customer life cycle below, write *one* action step you can implement in your business to include this step in your operations.

1. Drive Traffic

_____

_____

_____

_____

2. Capture Data

_____

_____

_____

_____

3. Nurture Leads

_____

_____

_____

_____

4. Convert Sales

_____

_____

_____

_____

_____

_____

5. Deliver and WOW!

_____

_____

_____

_____

_____

_____

6. Upsell

_____

_____

_____

_____

_____

_____

7. Refer Others

_____

_____

_____

_____

_____

As you finish this chapter, do you have any final thoughts or questions about Life Cycle Marketing?

_____

_____

_____

_____

_____

_____

_____

In your own words, explain the importance of an automated system in helping you move clients along this life cycle.

_____

_____

_____

_____

_____

_____

_____

chapter 7

BRINGING YOUR MESSAGE TO MARKET

In order to bring your message to market most effectively, you need to capitalize on each one of the following phases so that they work together in harmony.

Read Chapter 7 in *Unleashed*

Reflect and Discuss

"What I haven't seen is a comprehensive approach that combines all these components into one master plan."

Respond

Why do you think many leaders (and leadership consultants) focus on only one or a few of these phases?

_____

_____

_____

_____

In your own words, explain why it's crucial to have excellence in each one.

_____

_____

_____

_____

Which of Martijn's questions on page 70 resonate with you? Why do you think that is?

_____

_____

_____

_____

Respond

How do you find yourself modeling your organization or personal brand after others?

_____

_____

_____

_____

_____

_____

_____

What positive things have you found from imitating others?

_____

_____

_____

_____

_____

_____

_____

_____

Have you seen any negative results from it?

_____

_____

_____

_____

_____

_____

_____

_____

What innovative ideas or steps are you implementing that are uniquely your own?

_____

_____

_____

_____

_____

_____

_____

_____

What positive results have you found in innovation?

_____

_____

_____

_____

_____

_____

_____

_____

_____

Respond

Do you agree with this statement? Explain your answer.

_____

_____

_____

_____

_____

_____

_____

How many categories do you think God has for His people? What does your answer mean for you and your purpose?

_____

_____

_____

_____

_____

_____

_____

_____

What are your thoughts on Martijn's Optimization vs. Innovation diagram on p. 76?

_____

_____

_____

_____

_____

_____

_____

_____

_____

_____

"Innovation is not just limited to phase one. It's something that needs to be applied throughout all the phases."

Respond

In your own words, what does this statement mean for your brand or business?

_____

_____

_____

_____

_____

_____

_____

Are there any ideas or action steps you want to implement in your life after reading this chapter?

_____

_____

_____

_____

_____

_____

_____

UNLEASHED: Study Guide | 63

chapter 8

IDENTIFY

Knowing who you are in Christ is the most important and most difficult part of this process. We start with identity and purpose.

Read Chapter 8 in *Unleashed*

Reflect and Discuss

Everything starts with identifying your message. What is the unique value proposition God has given you? What value does your calling bring to those around you?

Respond

How would you answer these questions in this season of your life?

_____

_____

_____

_____

Why do you think many high-level influencers struggle to answer this question?

_____

_____

_____

_____

How does it make you feel to know that your message doesn't need to be one-size-fits-all or appeal to everyone?

_____

_____

_____

_____

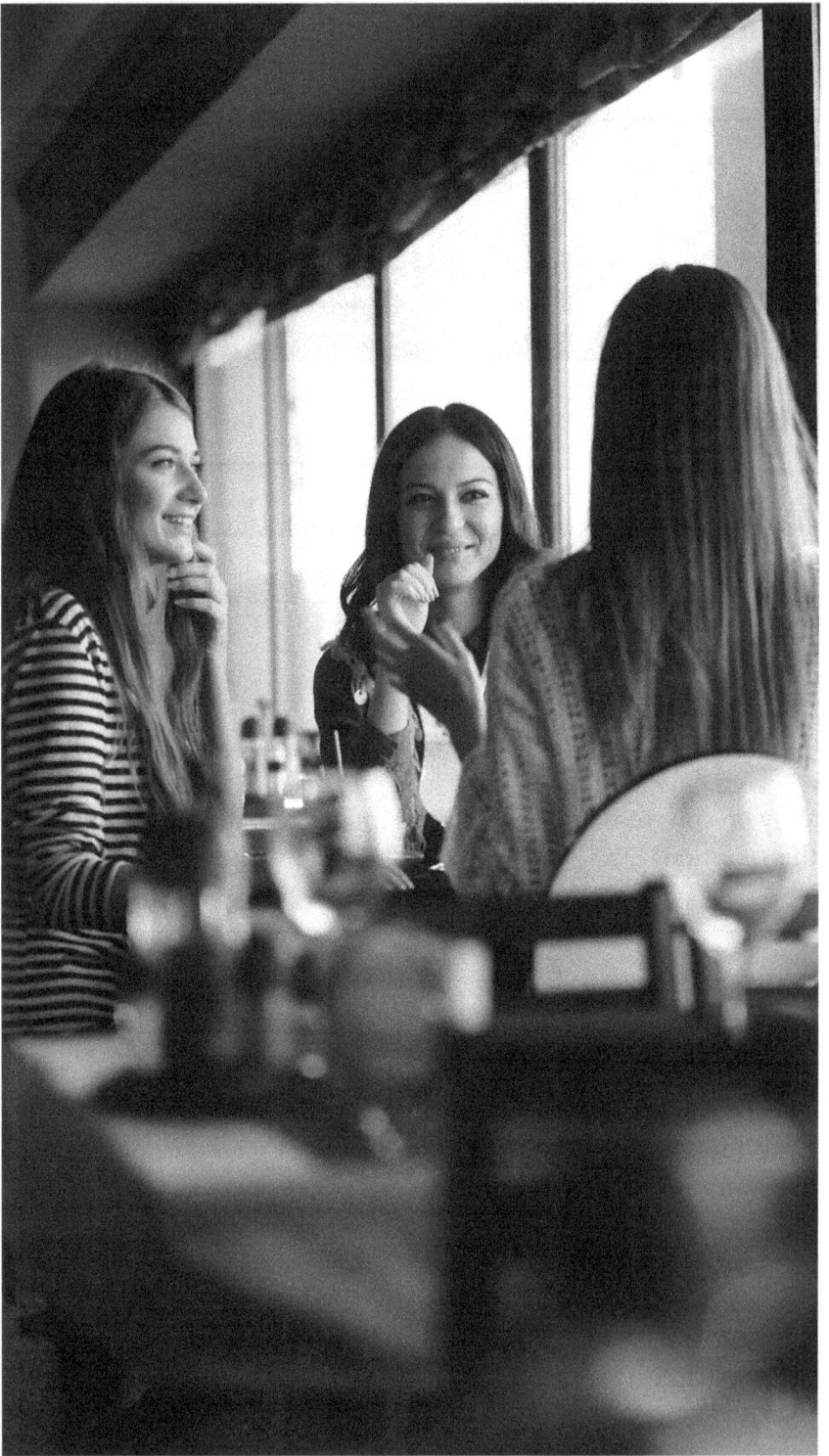

Reflect and Discuss

"[Jesus] knew His target audience: the ones who would most benefit from the value He was offering. He knew they were the poor, the brokenhearted, the captives, the blind, and the oppressed."

Respond

Who is your target audience? Who will benefit the most from what you have to offer?

_____

_____

_____

_____

_____

_____

_____

How are you going after this audience right now? Are you satisfied with your current ability to reach them?

_____

_____

_____

_____

_____

_____

Reflect and Discuss

"There are so many sides to God's creative expression that it's impossible for one human to display them. In fact, collectively as humanity, we still aren't able to define the boundaries of His creative expression: He does more than what we can even think or imagine."

Respond

Who do you know who reveals a different side of God's creative expression than you do? What do they show the world of Him?

_____

_____

_____

_____

_____

_____

How might your ministry, business, or personal life be limited by man-made templates?

_____

_____

_____

_____

_____

_____

Why do you think we create these templates so often?

_____

_____

_____

_____

_____

_____

_____

Reflect and Discuss

"We model after each other instead of trying to figure out who God says we are individually. The devil will make you believe uniformity is a virtue, but it isn't. It may have the appearance of godliness, but it has denied the power thereof."

Respond

In your own words, explain the difference between unity and uniformity.

_____

_____

_____

_____

_____

_____

What importance does diversity hold for your life and/or organization?

_____

_____

_____

_____

_____

_____

_____

How do you see God's diverse design exemplified in Scripture?

_____

_____

_____

_____

_____

_____

_____

"For the first time in his life, Peter had a revelation about who he was supposed to be, as Jesus Himself identified him by uttering words of destiny and purpose over his life."

Respond

What unique identity has God given you? What has He spoken over your life in particular?

_____

_____

_____

_____

_____

_____

_____

How does your God-given identity connect to what God says about Himself?

_____

_____

_____

_____

_____

_____

_____

Why do you think the church often stops short of acknowledging this level of revelation?

_____

_____

_____

_____

_____

_____

_____

Respond

Have you identified some, or all, of these essential things?

_____

_____

_____

_____

_____

_____

_____

What do you still need to find out?

_____

_____

_____

_____

_____

_____

_____

chapter 9

PACKAGE

The power of our message isn't just in the message itself, but in how we package and present it to the public. Stepping outside of traditional publishing models opens up doors for innovation and an increase in profitability.

Read Chapter 9 in *Unleashed*

Reflect and Discuss

"I'm convinced that everyone has information that can help answer others' questions. It's simply a matter of identifying that knowledge and making it available for consumption."

Respond

What information do you possess that can help answer others' questions, concerns, or problems?

_____

_____

_____

_____

What kind of people could benefit the most from the message you have to share?

_____

_____

_____

_____

Who has spoken into your life and given you the tools and wisdom you needed at that time?

_____

_____

_____

_____

"Many Christian influencers are broke because they haven't packed their information in an innovative and strategic way."

Respond

Why do you think the majority of faith communities only focus on preaching and book writing, instead of making use of other media?

_____

_____

_____

_____

_____

_____

_____

What unique ways of packaging information could you use in the future that you haven't taken advantage of to date?

_____

_____

_____

_____

_____

_____

_____

How could utilizing the methods you listed above, or the ones Martijn lists in the book, significantly cut your costs and production time?

_____

_____

_____

_____

_____

_____

Does this chapter change your perspective of books and book writing? Explain your answer.

_____

_____

_____

_____

_____

_____

"Your audience's engagement with a product on the lower levels of the ladder will lead them to the next level of financial engagement."

Respond

What are the "lower levels" of your ladder currently—those products or services that don't cost the member or customer a lot?

_____

_____

_____

_____

_____

_____

Do you have any "higher rungs" in place—costlier options that provide higher value to the customer and more profit for you?

_____

_____

_____

_____

_____

_____

_____

Based on your answers above, which do you need to focus more on developing—low-level options or high-level options?

_____

_____

_____

_____

_____

_____

_____

"Publishers (and most authors) center their strategy solely around the book, instead of the message. There is no ladder. There is only a book."

Respond

What are the inherent dangers of placing all of your strategizing and capital into only one product?

_____

_____

_____

_____

_____

_____

Might the traditional publishing model appeal to customers? Is it possible that it won't?

_____

_____

_____

_____

_____

_____

Why do you think more people are interested in something free than in buying something at regular price?

_____

_____

_____

_____

_____

_____

Do you have any questions or thoughts about the marketing funnel Martijn discusses?

_____

_____

_____

_____

_____

_____

chapter 10

DISTRIBUTE YOUR BRAND/MESSAGE

If we want people to buy into our message, we first need our message to be heard. We need to make sure we have a vehicle that allows us to "preach" our message to our target audience.

Read Chapter 10 in *Unleashed*

Respond

What's the value of YOUR message? How will it impact people's lives for the better?

_____

_____

_____

_____

_____

Who can benefit most from the value you have to offer?

_____

_____

_____

_____

_____

Where can you find these people in large numbers?

_____

_____

_____

_____

_____

_____

_____

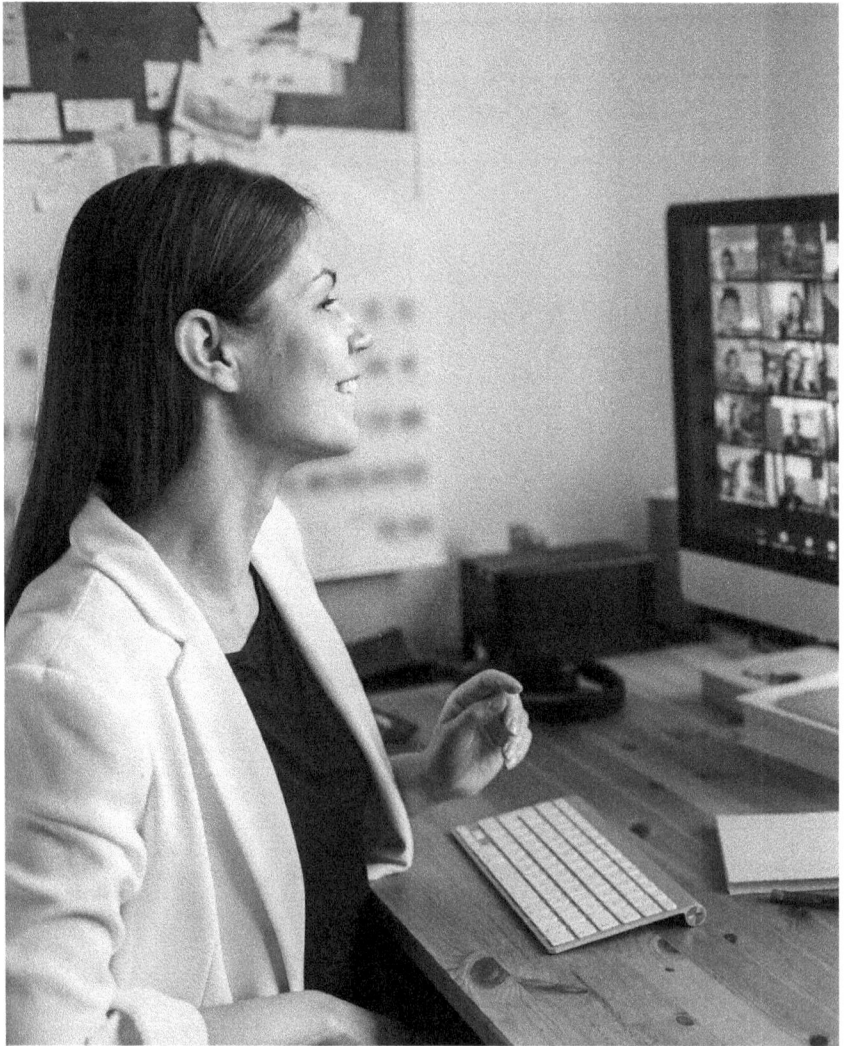

Reflect and Discuss

"If you want to reach people, you have to reach them where they spend time."

Respond

Where does your audience spend time? On what platforms and media are they most often found?

_____

_____

_____

_____

Which spaces are you already inhabiting that your audience also enjoys?

_____

_____

_____

_____

Which platforms do you need to research and get involved in more?

_____

_____

_____

_____

Respond

What value can you offer to your audience on the platforms they frequent?

_____

_____

_____

_____

_____

_____

_____

How can social media platforms help you demonstrate the value and benefit that you have to offer?

_____

_____

_____

_____

_____

_____

_____

How might using platforms to add value create a situation for you where your customers begin to buy from you as if it were their own idea?

_____

_____

_____

_____

_____

_____

_____

"Most influencers create content; they just don't repurpose it well. Content needs to be packaged in the right format to be compatible with the platform."

Respond

Are you currently repurposing any of your content in secondary ways? If so, what are you using it for?

_____

_____

_____

_____

_____

_____

_____

Reading over Martijn's list of repurposing ideas on p. 113, what are some formats or packaging methods that might serve you well?

_____

_____

_____

_____

_____

_____

_____

Why is it essential to understand the culture of each platform you promote on?

_____

_____

_____

_____

_____

_____

_____

Are you good about replying to interactions on your social media content? Explain your answer.

_____

_____

_____

_____

_____

_____

What new opportunities, platforms, and strategies do you see on the horizon that you may be able to use in the days soon to come?

_____

_____

_____

_____

_____

chapter 11

ADVERTISE

Advertising is about creating a moment in front of your target audience. This moment is an opportunity to tell your story, engage a new audience, and introduce it to what you have to offer.

Read Chapter 11 in *Unleashed*

Reflect and Discuss

"There are distinct differences between branding, advertising, and marketing. These three words are often used interchangeably, yet they are each unique."

Respond

In your own words, explain the difference between branding, advertising, and marketing.

_____

_____

_____

_____

Which of these elements are you doing well with and paying attention to?

_____

_____

_____

_____

Which of these elements do you need to pay more attention to?

_____

_____

_____

_____

Reflect and Discuss

"Advertising serves as a conversion point that turns your audience's attention into a campaign (or funnel). While you're out there telling your story on all these platforms, you want there to be a moment when you convert that attention into this process. An effective ad allows you to do just that."

Respond

What new audiences can become available to you through advertising? What groups of people can you reach that weren't in your circle of influence before?

_____

_____

_____

_____

_____

_____

How does it make you feel to know that, no matter your current audience size, advertising can help it grow?

_____

_____

_____

_____

_____

_____

_____

According to God's Word, what's His perspective on beginnings and the small things?

_____

_____

_____

_____

_____

_____

_____

"Most traditional media platforms seduce you with outrageous vanity metrics. Their true reach is significantly less than what they will promise you in their media kits."

Respond

Why are metrics so important?

_____

_____

_____

_____

_____

_____

_____

What dangers are there in not tracking your content's performance on the platforms you use?

_____

_____

_____

_____

_____

_____

_____

How can you contextualize your message for your audience more effectively?

_____

_____

_____

_____

_____

_____

_____

Respond

We're always more effective together than we are alone. Who do you know who has influence in places you do not?

_____

_____

_____

_____

_____

_____

What influence do you have to offer to this person's audience that they don't already possess? What value (a service or product) can you offer them?

_____

_____

_____

_____

_____

_____

What are some ideas for collaborations, affiliations, or relationships you can build with others? What projects, events, or other partnerships can you brainstorm together?

_____

_____

_____

_____

_____

_____

_____

chapter 12

MARKETING

*"Your campaign is really about engaging
your audience in such a way that they
start pursuing you for what you have,
instead of you pursuing them. Sales, then,
becomes the automatic by-product of an
effective, well-developed campaign."*

Read Chapter 12 in *Unleashed*

Reflect and Discuss

"We simply must demonstrate that our information and services move people from pain to pleasure."

Respond

How does the information and insight you have to share in your message move people from pain to pleasure?

_____

_____

_____

_____

_____

In your own words, explain the Escape and Arrival Principle.

_____

_____

_____

_____

How can you *show* people that what you have to offer will move them from pain to pleasure?

_____

_____

_____

_____

Reflect and Discuss

"Jesus didn't try to 'sell' Nicodemus the gospel message until Nicodemus pursued Him."

Respond

How does it make you feel to know that Jesus wasn't trying to "sell" the gospel 24/7 to every single person He came across?

_____

_____

_____

_____

_____

_____

_____

What does this mean for you in your business, personal brand, or project?

_____

_____

_____

_____

_____

_____

_____

Take a look at Martijn's diagram on p. 139 and the subsequent struggles and benefits lists. Now, develop a diagram and set of lists based on your own value proposition. Make sure to include the pain points, outcomes, and steps in the process!

_____

_____

_____

_____

_____

_____

_____

How can you identify with the struggles of your audience?

_____

_____

_____

_____

_____

_____

What external and internal struggles can you tell your audience about to better connect with their pain points?

_____

_____

_____

_____

_____

_____

What's your "epiphany" point? How can you effectively share it with your audience?

_____

_____

_____

_____

_____

_____

Respond

Why is it so important to make sure your audience members have consumed your lead magnet before moving on to the next step in the sales cycle?

_____

_____

_____

_____

_____

_____

_____

Why does one-size-fits-all communication typically not work?

_____

_____

_____

_____

_____

_____

_____

How can you better tailor your communication to certain members of your audience?

_____

_____

_____

_____

_____

_____

_____

chapter 13

SELL

A sales funnel is more of a three-dimensional website, that allows a prospect to move deeper into the sales cycles by taking micro-steps forward into the funnel.

Read Chapter 13 in *Unleashed*

Respond

In your own words, explain the difference between a traditional webpage and a sales funnel page.

_____

_____

_____

_____

What benefits does a sales funnel page provide that a traditional website does not?

_____

_____

_____

_____

Do you see any potential downsides to a sales funnel page?

_____

_____

_____

_____

Which option do you think works best for your specific value proposition, product line, and service options? Explain your answer.

_____

_____

_____

_____

_____

_____

_____

Reflect and Discuss

"Subscriptions allow you to build monthly cash flow like no other type of product, because you know that every month (or year), your subscription automatically renews and collects money on your behalf."

Respond

Do you currently have a paid subscription plan for your members?

_____

_____

_____

_____

_____

_____

Is a subscription plan something you would consider implementing into your sales process? Why or why not?

_____

_____

_____

_____

_____

_____

Reflect and Discuss

"Innovation requires change. Change is hard. However, if you always do what you've always done, you'll always get what you've always gotten!"

Respond

What "red tape," or traditional practices, may be holding you back from embracing change?

_____

_____

_____

_____

_____

_____

Are you part of a larger organization or a smaller company? How does this affect the amount of red tape you have to go through to get things done?

_____

_____

_____

_____

_____

_____

In your own words, what does it mean to be "unreasonable"?

_____

_____

_____

_____

_____

_____

_____

chapter 14

DELIVER YOUR PRODUCT

We should always overdeliver. Sweeten the deal. Give more than what we promised. This gives us leverage.

Read Chapter 14 in *Unleashed*

Reflect and Discuss

"For each product, the question is the same: 'How do I get this to my customer in a user-friendly way that doesn't allow others to steal my stuff?'"

Respond

Make a list of each of the major products and services you offer. Then, jot down any ideas or practices you've used in delivering those things. Are there any processes that need updating? Circle these.

_____

_____

_____

_____

_____

_____

Look at the products/processes that you circled above. Based on Martijn's suggestions, what changes or updates can you begin to research and implement?

_____

_____

_____

_____

_____

_____

Do you have any other big takeaways or revelations from reading this chapter?

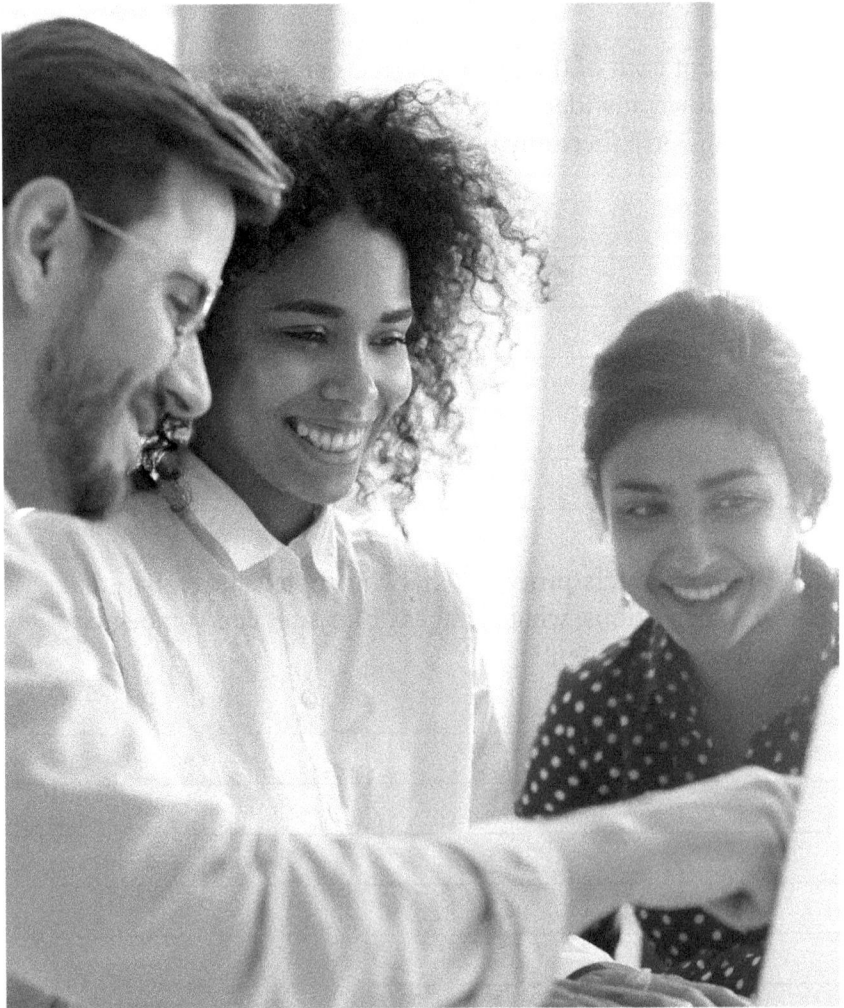

_____

_____

_____

_____

_____

_____

_____

chapter 15

WHAT DO I DO NEXT?

As we close, remember that everything in this book is simple, but that doesn't mean it will be easy. It will require commitment, perseverance, and hard work.

Read Chapter 15 in *Unleashed*

Reflect and Discuss

"You are unique. Your message is unique. What you bring to the table is new. Therefore, you are an innovator. There is no other point of reference for what you have. God gave you a gift that was uniquely picked out by Him for you."

Respond

As you finish this book, how are you feeling?

_____

_____

_____

_____

_____

_____

What takeaways stand out to you most from your experience?

_____

_____

_____

_____

_____

_____

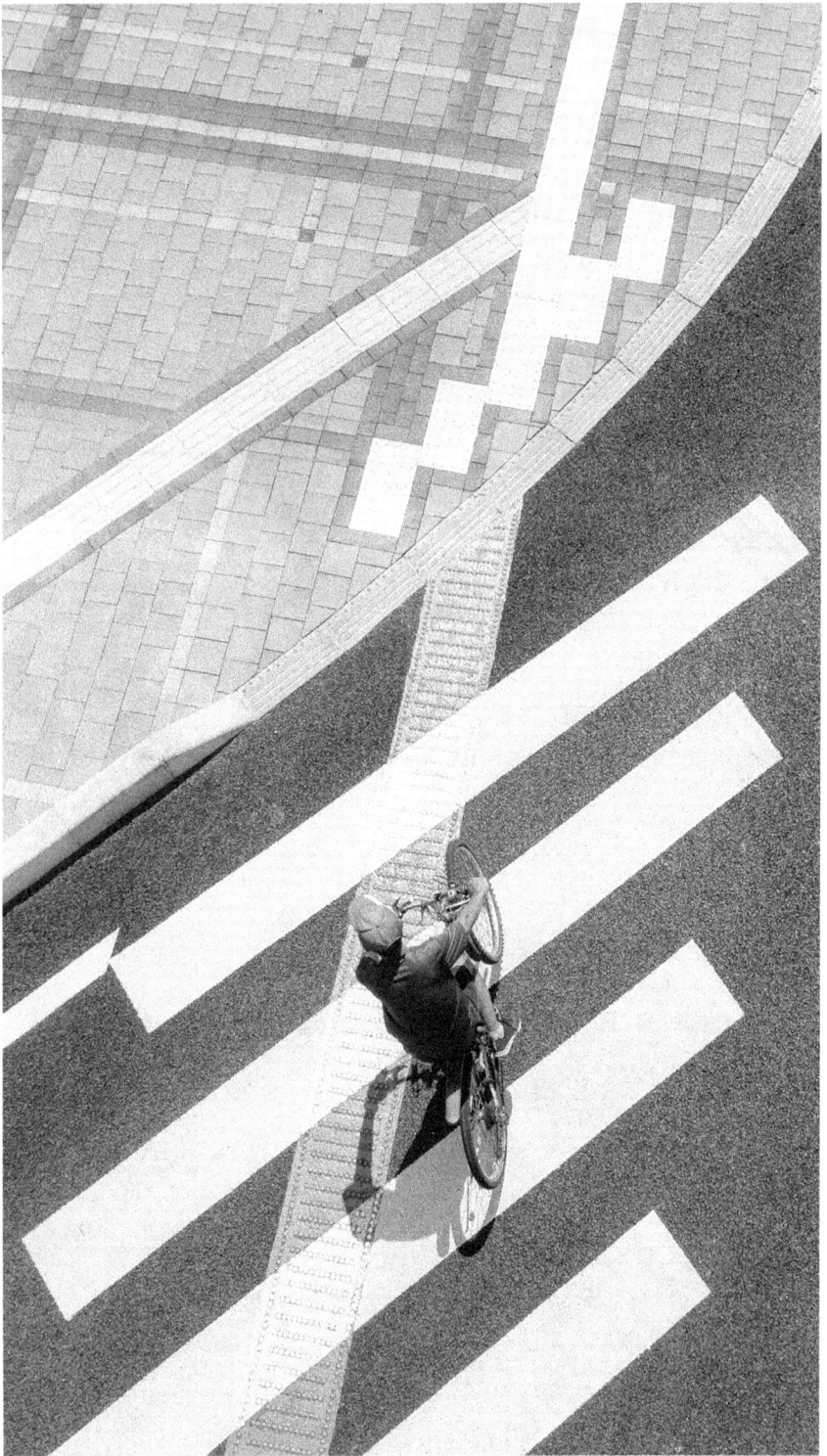

What questions, concerns, or reservations do you still have?

_____

_____

_____

_____

_____

_____

What's one thing you can implement in your life that can help you become unleashed?

_____

_____

_____

_____

_____

_____

ABOUT THE AUTHOR

Martijn van Tilborgh is a marketing architect, speaker, author, and serial entrepreneur.

He consults with countless large organizations and well known individuals, and has also launched many of his own products successfully. He is always looking to create the NEXT BIG THING in the different niches he works in.

He, his wife Amy, and his three kids reside in Orlando, Florida.